COPING

I0812630

BODY SHAMING

ROSE MCCARTHY

ROSEN PUBLISHING

Published in 2023 by The Rosen Publishing Group, Inc.
2544 Clinton Street, Buffalo, NY 14224

Portions of this work were originally authored by Natalie Chomet and published as *Coping with Body Shaming*. All new material in this edition was authored by Rose McCarthy.

Designer: Rachel Rising
Editor: Corona Brezina

Library of Congress Cataloging-in-Publication Data

Names: McCarthy, Rose
Title: Body shaming / Rose McCarthy.
Description: New York : Rosen, 2023. | Series: Coping|
Includes bibliographic references, index and glossary.
Identifiers: ISBN 9781499473629 (pbk) | ISBN 9781499473636
(library bound) | ISBN 9781499473643 (ebook)
Subjects: LCSH: Body image--Juvenile literature.
| Mind and body --Juvenile literature.
Classification: LCC BF175.5.B64 M33 2023 | DDC 306.4--dc23

Manufactured in the United States of America

CPSIA Compliance Information: Batch #CSRYA23. For further information, contact Rosen Publishing at 1-800-237-9932.

CONTENTS

CHAPTER 1

A CULTURE OF SHAMING

Can you remember an instance in which you were body shamed? Maybe somebody laughed at your clothes or hurled a derogatory insult at you. There's no easy way to describe the pain of humiliation you feel when being shamed. It's a powerful emotion that's hard to forget.

In traditional societies, shame served a useful purpose. Shaming people for bad behavior helped enforce social expectations. If children were shamed for misbehavior, they learned proper cultural norms. By seeing other people shamed, people learned the consequences of breaking the rules.

But in modern times, shaming has turned toxic. Instead of being shamed for improper actions, people are often shamed for who they are as human beings. In earlier times, a person living in a small community could learn from the shaming and move past it. Today, a person can be shamed on the internet by huge numbers of strangers. Due to the prevalence of social media, public shaming can haunt people for long after the incident.

Body shaming is directed at people on the basis of physical appearance. People are shamed over their weight, age, facial features, and skin tone. They're criticized for their hygiene, clothing, or attractiveness. Today, there's no constructive purpose to such shaming. It serves only to make people feel bad about themselves.

SHAPING AN UNREALISTIC IDEAL

In modern American society, women are subject to pressure to conform to many beauty ideals that seem nearly impossible to exist in one single body at once: small waist, large breasts (but not too large), a gap between skinny thighs, but also a curvy backside (but not too prominent). If women all believed they needed to have every one of these attributes, who wouldn't look in the mirror and find they came up short?

It isn't only girls and women who are often dissatisfied with their bodies. Boys and men feel the pressure too. For both girls and guys, the overexposure to images of bodies considered to be ideal takes its toll on body image and self-esteem. Boys and men are increasingly unhappy with their own bodies for one reason or another. Many trans people also experience discomfort regarding their own body, and it can be difficult for them to navigate unrealistic societal expectations of beauty based largely on two genders.

Teens in particular are in a position to feel less than satisfied with how they look since they're still developing and getting used to their changing bodies themselves. And often, putting others down is an easy

Media images portray the ideal male body as more muscular than it's possible for most men to achieve—sometimes called the "superhero effect" influenced by movies.

way to give yourself a quick boost of self-esteem. It's also a form of social bonding, but the quick surge is more of a Band-Aid on the problem than a solution. You won't feel great about yourself just by making others feel worse. And chances are, if the bonds of friendship you form with your social circle are mainly based on superficiality, they're going to prove awfully breakable in the end. So between cultural norms, the awkwardness of puberty, and social pressure, how can you combat them all and feel good in your own skin? The first step is identifying the sources of body shame.

Our society shapes our expectations and opinions on what defines a beautiful or merely acceptable body. Media as well as the behavior of those around us start to shape these perceptions early in childhood. Many studies have shown that kids as young as three or four years old are already afraid of getting fat.

From a young age, children start to absorb messages about standards of beauty and body image from the people and media sources around them.

RETOUCHED TO EXTREMES

It's no secret that celebrity images are often digitally altered in magazines and other media. Photos are frequently retouched to remove blemishes from skin, make bodies appear slimmer, and erase signs of aging. Publications often release these photos without consulting the subject about the changes, and some celebrities have been outspoken in criticizing the alterations in their appearance.

Actress Kate Winslet has repeatedly taken a stand against digital image manipulation. In 2015, she negotiated an ad contract with L'Oréal stipulating that her features would not be retouched. While filming the acclaimed 2021 TV series *Mare of Easttown* she refused to let the director slim down her belly in a filmed scene and rejected promo posters that appeared overly retouched.

Other celebrities, however, embrace digital alterations. Some celebrity social media accounts are notorious for posting manipulated images.

Actress Kate Winslet was body shamed about her weight after her breakout role in the movie *Titanic*, released in 1997. Today, she's known for promoting body acceptance.

The images we are exposed to each day in the media perpetuate beauty ideals that are often physically impossible. Imagine you are traveling to school in the morning. If you take public transit, you may find your eyes resting on an ad in your bus or train car. By car, you'll likely pass billboards that depict models posing in unnatural ways or celebrities whose features appear smooth and flawless. Stop at a deli or newsstand to get a pack of gum or a snack and you're confronted with countless magazine covers touting swimsuit-clad supermodels or boasting about a new thirteen-day, fat-busting miracle diet.

Next time you see an image on an ad or magazine cover, ask yourself, what's wrong with this picture? Nearly all of the images that bombard our conscious and subconscious minds each day are altered to achieve the supposed perfection we find ourselves striving for in real life. Instead of doing this through diet and exercise or even surgery, these bodies are enhanced digitally.

DIFFERENT PLACES, DIFFERENT TIMES, DIFFERENT STANDARDS

Pressure to look a certain way doesn't come only from images in the media. Whether it's the aspects of your appearance your family praises the most or the way your mom talks about her own body, your own conceptions of what's beautiful and what's not start to form early and may come from your own home. Family dynamics can play a large part in how you see yourself.

Even young children receive subtle pressure from online media sources about how they should aspire to look and behave according to certain standards for beauty.

Think of home in a broader sense. The overall culture of Western civilization today sees skinny as beautiful and muscular as handsome. But in other parts of the world, the standards of beauty are not the same. In Brazil, for example, a curvy, tanned woman is considered beautiful—perhaps too curvy or not slim enough by current American standards. In Japan, women with crooked teeth are considered cute and youthful. (You can even buy dentures to achieve the look!) And, believe it or not, surgery bandages indicating a recent nose job are worn with pride by women in Iran.

The aesthetics of what looks good to us is more than a case of taste. It is often an indication of what current society values. A quick scan of America through time can show how these ideals changed along with what was going on in the world: in the 1910s, the androgynous, thin flapper was attractive during a time when women were fighting for the right to vote; in the 1950s, Marilyn Monroe's curvy figure that emphasized the feminine was the beauty ideal when Americans were experiencing the post–World War II economic boom.

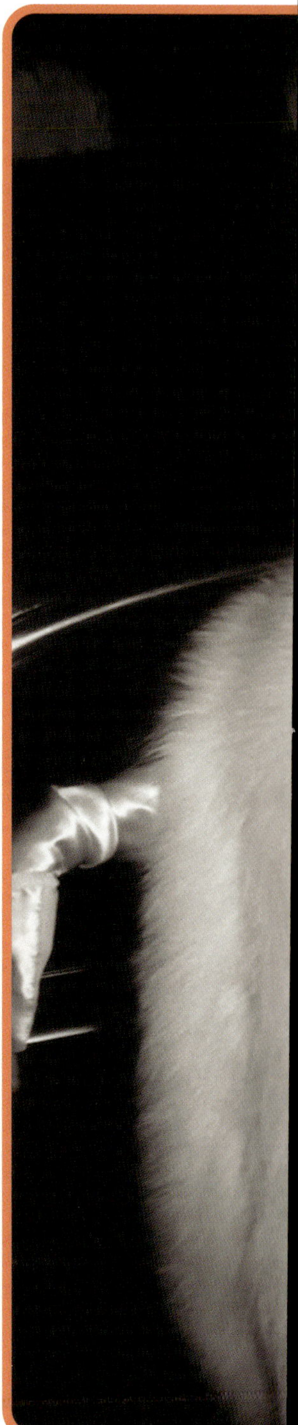

Would iconic actress Marilyn Monroe be body shamed today? Many women consider the modern ideal body shape to be thinner and more toned.

There may be some sociological reasons why we gravitate toward people who look like us and, by extension, shun or ignore those who appear different in some way. In early times, our survival depended on banding together for protection and strength. The ability to tell the difference between friend and foe was distilled to quick categorizations. We assessed the people around us to see if we were alike in obvious, fundamental ways and therefore "friends." These quick groupings of friends and enemies were often based on appearance. Today, our social identities are often shaped by what we have in common with the people around us. Though our survival no longer depends on it, we still try to conform to those around us to fit in socially. Some of those groupings may be based on religion, where you grew up, and common interests or hobbies. Many others may unconsciously still be based on appearance. Have you ever noticed that the kids that sit alone at lunch are often the ones who are considered different in some way?

Body shaming can feel particularly cruel during adolescence, when young people are exploring their identities and trying to figure out where they fit in. To an insecure teenager, every small perceived flaw can seem like a catastrophe that could leave them ostracized by their peers. Thoughtless body shaming comments can make them even more self-conscious and vulnerable. Persistent body shaming can have serious mental and physical health consequences.

You can't necessarily stop people from body shaming. But you can refuse to allow body shaming to define who you are or decide what qualities you value in yourself and other people. You can learn to practice kindness and respect toward your own body and avoid joining in body shaming of others.

You can reject body shaming by refusing to judge others—or yourself—based solely on appearance without bothering to look any deeper.

CHAPTER 2

SOURCES OF SHAMING

It might sometimes seem like there's no safe space from body shaming. At school, students are subjected to teasing and bullying. Sometimes people intend to hurt their target, but the pain can be even worse when a friend or peer unintentionally or offhandedly shames your appearance. Online, many people feel free to unleash hateful comments that they'd never utter in real life. It's hurtful to receive insults personally, of course, but it can also be difficult to see public figures and celebrities that you admire subjected to poisonous attacks about their bodies. Sometimes, even family members can be body shamers. Many adults with body weight issues, for example, can recall how a parent discouraged them from taking second helpings or praised them for losing weight as they grew up. These parents generally have their kids' interests at heart—they want to raise beautiful, healthy children. But they don't realize that discouraging eating can contribute to an adolescent developing an unhealthy relationship with food, or that praising weight loss can contribute to a lifelong pattern of weight fluctuation accompanied by guilt.

PEERS AND PRESSURE

There's a reason the schoolyard bully is a cliché: kids can be cruel, and everyone has experienced what it feels like to be on the tail end of a joke or insult at school or among peers. Going through adolescence comes with a unique set of pressures. Though there are the obvious ones that come from your family and your school to do well and be successful, there are also the many pressures of finding a niche or group of friends where you are liked and accepted. For most, this translates

Many teens would rather blend in and conform to accepted standards of behavior and appearance than stand out from the crowd and risk being bullied or body shamed.

to fitting in or simply trying not to stand out too much. Because of the way family and society shape us, by the time kids reach their teen years they have a set idea of what normal means, and more often than not, it's easier and more appealing to blend in and conform to those standards than to break the ranks.

Fitting in may sound easy enough, but a problem arises when someone's body does not conform with what peers consider normal. You don't have to actively bully people for looking different to make them feel bad. Not standing up for them or deciding to take the easy route and not socialize with them just perpetuates the problem.

It's easy to stand quietly by or make a comment or joke when someone is being shamed for looking different. The human brain doesn't fully form until we hit our twenties, and our identities and personalities are still shaping too. Add a surge of hormones and you've got a volatile recipe for personal insecurities. Being aware that everyone is worried about seeming cool and having friends can give some context to why body shaming happens—especially with other teens.

VIRTUAL IMAGES, REAL SHAME

We live in a time when people regularly take to the internet as a way to freely share their opinions without fear of consequence, so it follows that body shaming often takes place virtually. Anonymity makes it easier to say whatever comes to mind, and the lack of face-to-face confrontation means that the shamers don't have to see or acknowledge the results of their words. Add to the mix a heaping dose of imagery of bodies displayed online—from selfies to dating profile pictures to celebrity photos—and you have plenty of openings for anyone to pick someone else's appearance apart. To make matters worse, many body-related "challenges" quickly start trending online and encourage people to post pictures of parts of their body to see if they are acceptable or ideal according to unrealistic standards.

People are posting more images of themselves online than ever before, but they're also potentially exposing themselves to body shaming and other hostile reactions.

CELEBS SPEAK OUT

The acclaimed musician Billie Eilish rose to fame at a young age, touring as a headlining artist while still a teenager. Eilish has received hateful online criticism for her body shape and her clothing choices. Instead of accepting the abuse, Eilish has challenged her attackers in her songs and videos. Eilish has been open about her body image issues and addressed her experiences with body shaming in the 2020 short film *Not My Responsibility*.

Eilish has asserted that "the internet hates women," but men aren't exempt from body shaming either. In 2021, the comedic actor Jonah Hill opened up about his body insecurity, stating that he didn't feel comfortable being shirtless in front of others until he was in his mid-30s. He also requested on his social media account that people refrain from commenting on his body.

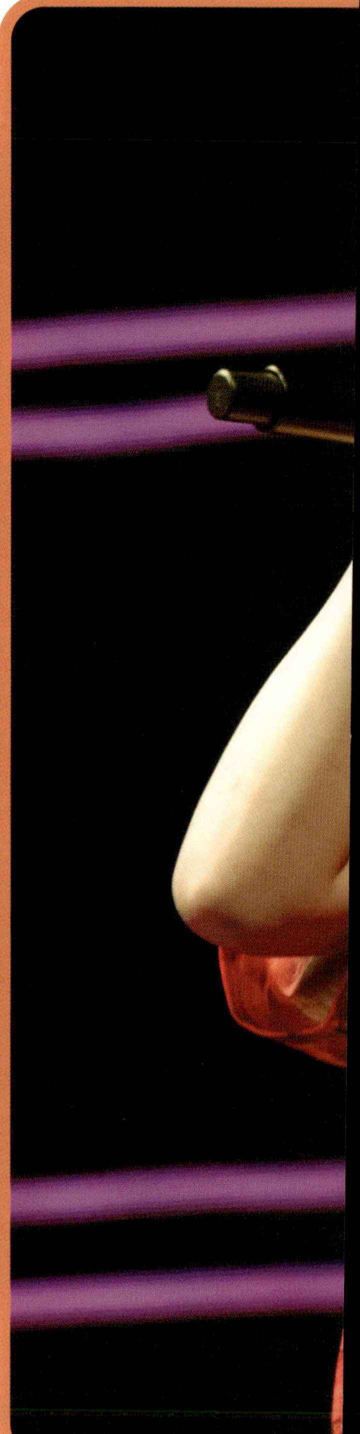

Born in 2001, Billie Eilish has had numerous hit albums and singles, and she was the youngest person ever to win all four major Grammy awards in the same year.

STAYING AUTHENTIC AND POSITIVE

Is there an upshot to the digital discourse about our bodies that seems to never stop? Body-positive narratives attempt to counter the shaming. People famous and unknown have posted video responses, images with captions, hashtags, and entire blogs devoted to combating body shaming and promoting body positivity. Whether a post addresses specific shamers and calls them out for adding their toxic voice to the world or simply shows someone who is comfortable in his or her own skin, these efforts have made body shaming a public conversation. For every voice that speaks up against body shaming online, there could be dozens of others who see that and take solace in the fact that the narrative is changing.

Have you ever been in a relationship or had a crush on someone who caused you to feel that his or her affection depended on you looking a certain way? Whether it's how the person treated you or actual things he or she said, the feeling remained that you had to be skinny enough/muscled enough/tall enough (you get the idea) to be worthy of attention and love.

These toxic dynamics can occur subconsciously and unintentionally. The person you're dating could make you feel that you should be satisfied with whatever you get, whether it's cold detachment or emotional abuse, because he or she has made you believe that you cannot find anything better. It probably speaks more to that person's lack of self-confidence that he or she has to make you feel small and unworthy of affection, in order to have power.

It can be difficult to remain positive and confident when you're in a relationship with someone who makes you feel like you're not worthy of them.

Having strong friendships can serve to counter body shaming messages by showing what sorts of qualities really matter in the people who are close to you.

Friends can do this just as easily as romantic partners can. Solid friendships affirm your self-worth and confidence, while a toxic friendship that focuses on negativity will make both parties feel worse about themselves. It can be hard to maintain an overall positive attitude when you're going through a time in your life where your body, hormones, brain, and identity are still developing and changing. But mutually supportive friendships, relationships, and communities do exist, and you can build them yourself. Notice what your friends or your date spends a lot of time talking about. Is it dieting or how this shirt makes his arms look? Or is it the last episode of the show you both like to watch or that awesome concert coming up?

Perhaps you aren't in a relationship, but you feel that you can't meet someone who will want to date you until you make your body look a certain way, whether that means bulking up, losing a few pounds, or wearing the right kind of makeup or clothes. Though advertisements may lead us to believe that only certain body types are attractive or worthy of romantic attention, this is not the case in reality. No one, including yourself, should make you feel that your body is not good enough.

There's no easy one-size-fits-all response to body shaming. Online, it's often best to ignore hateful comments and block hostile users on social media, but you can't always ignore body shaming in real life. Depending on the situation, you may choose to tell a classmate that their statements make you feel uncomfortable or simply change the subject. If a friend frequently body shames you or others, you could have an honest talk with them about how their comments make you feel. You might decide that it's best to step back from a friendship if it threatens

Online body shaming might hurt, but you can close the app and choose to spend your time instead with friends who appreciate you for who you are.

MYTHS & FACTS

MYTH: Skinny people never feel shame about their bodies.

FACT: No matter their weight, everyone experiences shame about their body at some time or another. Our world today may prize being thin, but thinness does not directly correlate to having high self-esteem or a positive body image.

MYTH: Girls are more self-conscious about their bodies than boys.

FACT: Studies have shown that boys are more likely to see themselves as underweight or not muscular enough, while girls often obsess over thinness. A 2019 study found that almost a quarter of adolescent boys surveyed were unhappy with their bodies, even though they were a healthy weight. It goes to show that boys have anxiety about their bodies, too, and it may be more common than you think.

MYTH: I will feel better about my body when it's thinner/curvier/more muscled [fill in the blank].

FACT: That's not usually the case. If you want to lose weight, you may go on a diet and achieve your goal, but you may end up fixating on your weight even more than before. If your mind is trained to focus on your body's flaws (whatever you think they are), that's all you will see. You have to be happy with yourself as you are, and seeing the "right" number on a scale doesn't equal loving your body.

to turn toxic. Regardless of the circumstances, you should keep in mind that people's cruel and thoughtless body shaming comments don't define who you are.

CHAPTER 3

STRATEGIES FOR COPING

Body shaming cuts at the most vulnerable aspects of a person's core identity. An incident of body shaming often leaves the target feeling stunned and helpless, regardless of whether it occurs online or in person. But there are ways that you can respond that help you move past the shaming. Don't aim for revenge—there's little chance that you can inflict the same kind of hurt that you received, and exchanging insults won't help defuse an already toxic situation. But you may be able to share why you found a comment hurtful and convey to the other person the effects of body shaming. Over time, you may be able to shift body shaming habits among your friends and family. Most importantly, look after your own well-being. Think of the message behind Billie Eilish's lyrics, "Is my value based only on your perception? / Or is your opinion of me / Not my responsibility?" Other people don't define who you are as a person, and cruel comments shouldn't affect your sense of pride in your identity and accomplishments.

STANDING UP FOR YOURSELF

The idea of confronting someone who has just said something to hurt you can be daunting. But this doesn't mean you're picking a fight. There are several ways you can approach someone who has body shamed you, and most aim to defuse the situation. The simplest and most straightforward approach is explaining why a comment is hurtful. If a friend tells you the dress you tried on isn't flattering on your body type or if someone says your crush won't like you because you're not his or her type, calmly break down, in straightforward terms, why these words hurt you.

If a friend body shames you with a careless comment, explain why the words hurt you and ask them not to say those sorts of things in the future.

If you feel safe enough to do so, you can use the situation as a teachable moment. It could be an opportunity to explain what body positivity is, why it is important to you, and how you practice it in your life. It's easy to slip into the habit of criticizing your own body and those around you or focusing on the flaws as you have been trained to view them. If you feel comfortable enough to break this down for the person, then there's a good chance he or she could benefit from a dose of body positivity too.

Here's a tactic that is a little counterintuitive and may be difficult to do: sympathize. Can you contextualize this person for yourself and understand where some of the hurtful comments stem from? There are many reasons why people put others down, but more often than not, it has to do with something they are going through and less to do with you. Putting yourself in the other person's shoes may help take a little bit of the sting out of his or her actions. You'll come away with more awareness, poise, and compassion, and less of the hurt than before.

The simplest tactic and often the wisest one is to disengage. People who are body shaming you are looking for a response to show that what they have done has hurt you. If you don't give them anything back, they will run out of steam and you can walk away with your head held high. This choice will likely be the best option for dealing with those shamers who are combative or those who you know aren't worth the trouble. If this isn't someone you have a close relationship with, you won't lose much if you cut ties.

This tactic may also come into play when it comes to interactions with friends, family, and significant others. You have the right to decide that you don't want to go into a detailed explanation of why they hurt you or to have a tiring fight about it. If the person who has body shamed you is someone you want to stay close with, eventually you will have to confront him or her and try to repair the damage to your relationship, but that doesn't mean you have to do it as soon as the shaming occurs. Take the time you need to approach the situation with a level head. The best way to get over the pain of this is to let yourself experience the emotions that body shaming brings to the surface so that you can move through them and ultimately move on.

Body shaming hurts, and having a painful emotional response is normal. Try to be kind to yourself and move past the incident.

BODY POSITIVITY VS. BODY NEUTRALITY

The body positivity movement urges people to love their bodies regardless of its appearance. Some people, however, prefer to practice body neutrality, a perspective that focuses on the body's function rather than outward appearance. The body positivity movement emphasizes that everyone is beautiful in their own way. The body neutrality approach allows people to appreciate their body even if they consider it to possess imperfections. According to this mindset, people's self-worth shouldn't be dependent on the belief that they're beautiful. It's also more inclusive for some marginalized groups, such as trans people and people with disabilities, who may not love every aspect of their bodies.

The body neutrality movement involves treating your body with respect and valuing your body's capabilities. For some people, it's related to mindfulness, the practice of maintaining awareness of the present moment. Body neutrality emphasizes choosing food, clothing, and physical activities that make you feel good about yourself regardless of how they affect physical appearance. It also calls for respecting other people's bodies and refraining from shaming or criticism.

Actress Jameela Jamil is an advocate of the body neutrality movement, preferring to focus on her relationship, career, and friends rather than her own physical appearance.

NEGATIVE UNDERTONES

Sometimes body shaming isn't about the body being shamed at all. In order to break down negative comments about your body or someone else's, it helps to look deeper than the surface of the negative remark to what's at its root. It could be the low self-esteem of the person doing the shaming that's driving the negativity: putting you down to boost his or her own confidence, quieting insecurities, or even redirecting negative attention that could otherwise have been focused on him or her.

There are times when people use negative talk about someone's body as an easy excuse to voice criticisms about the person's character. If you notice this type of remark come up in conversation with someone you know, you can cut through the superficial by questioning the criticism: "What does weight/appearance have to do with what kind of person he is?" Even if a comment like that seems too direct, you can still steer the conversation to the actions or opinions that the person might take issue with rather than appearance-based remarks.

We know we will always have moments where we encounter negative body commentary, but knowing how to handle it when this kind of talk comes up is half the battle. Depending on the context and your comfort level, you can be up front about how that talk makes you feel, shift the conversation so that any remarks are focused on the actions or character of someone rather than his or her body, or give the shamer context to take away the power of his or her words.

PURPOSEFUL POSITIVITY

If someone is purposely saying hurtful things about your body, chanccs are the person wants a reaction. Whether it's to make you feel less worthy and humiliated or to get a cheap laugh from others, he or she is seeking a response. Instead of seeing a bully, if you can look at that person and see the insecurities that motivate the behavior, the shameful remarks might not pack the punch that they once did. Try to avoid fighting cruelty with more cruelty because no matter what your body looks like, no body type is free from issues of insecurity. Everyone has experienced shame at some time in their lives, skinny or not. All bodies are worthy of respect and kindness, and sinking to the level of someone who has body shamed you will just perpetuate the problem.

Besides the effect that body shaming may have on the person doing the shaming, it will likely take its toll on you too. The shamer may experience (or hope to experience) a brief boost in self-confidence in putting you down. The other effect his or her comments may have is to amplify or give voice to self-criticism in you that you might not have even been aware of before.

In dealing with shamers, don't let their negativity affect your own self-talk—the inner voice that reflects your thoughts about yourself and others. Don't dwell on cruel remarks about your body. You may not be able to control the people around you, but you can choose the things you tell yourself. You might find it difficult at first to dismiss body shaming and move on, but with practice, you can challenge these comments internally and replace them with positive self-messages. If you're able to reject body shaming in your own mind, you're demonstrating confidence that will help you succeed in many areas of your life.

Many people body shame themselves without realizing what they're doing. Don't let your own internal body shaming interfere with your enjoyment of life.

CHAPTER 4

RECOGNIZING BODY SHAMING

It's possible that the harshest body critic in your life is the person you see in the mirror. Many people engage in negative self-talk without realizing it. Have you ever caught a glance of your reflection and mentally criticized aspects of your own appearance? Do you make disparaging remarks about your weight after you've just enjoyed a good meal? Do you dread trying on clothes when shopping because you're sure that you'll look awful? Have you commented online about "before" and "after" diet photos? These types of self-messages will probably leave you feeling bad about yourself and your body. Try to recognize when you're shaming your own body and cut off negative self-talk.

Your comments about your own body and the bodies of others can influence the people around you too. By body shaming yourself, you're conveying the message that you don't think it's OK to be comfortable in your own body. If this attitude is common among your social group, your friends might join in body shaming themselves and others just to go along with everyone else. Try to break the body-shaming cycle by not obsessing on people's physical appearance, especially in critical terms.

Trying on clothes that don't fit can be frustrating and discouraging. Try to avoid focusing on your perceived flaws when you're shopping for clothes.

THE CONTAGION OF SHAME

Maybe you've made a comment about the "burrito baby" in your stomach after a lunch out to your favorite Mexican restaurant, said that you can't pull off a certain type of clothing because it's not flattering for your body type, or told someone you were going on a diet/exercise regimen to get a beach body or undo the damage from the holidays. At least one of these scenarios will likely seem familiar. If you've ever engaged in a conversation similar to one of these, you may be able to detect why it's detrimental to your own self-image, but what you may not be aware of is its effect on those around you.

When you put yourself down for a physical attribute that you see as a flaw, whether it's your weight, muscle mass, or body shape, you're communicating more than self-criticism. If you say to a friend, for example, "I feel fat," you're telling that friend a few things between the lines, one being that you think that it's bad to be fat. Though we are all most critical of ourselves, our talk about ourselves can be interpreted as how we see the people around us as well. Your own insecurity can validate the insecurities of those around you. If you tell your friends that you're not muscular enough, they'll see that as something you value, and if they aren't muscular either, their bodies won't be accepted as attractive or good enough either.

Even if you aren't saying something openly about someone else's body, you can still be implicitly commenting on it. For example, if you've commented that a certain item of clothing isn't flattering on you or on a friend's body, it may sound like you're talking about the item of clothing, but you're really talking about the person's body. You're implying that certain bodies are not supposed to wear this type of clothing while it's perfectly acceptable for other types of bodies to wear them. Putting it in these terms reveals how discriminatory and hurtful that can feel to the wearer.

Don't tell someone that a piece of clothing "isn't right" for them. It comes across as a criticism of their body, not of the clothing.

JUDGING BY APPEARANCES

Just as making comments about clothing being unflattering isn't about the clothes, the same applies to certain displays of concern for the health of others. A common misconception is that a person's fitness and health correspond directly to his or her weight. In reality, people of all shapes and sizes can be healthy—or unhealthy for that matter.

This is a common issue that many people may not even realize can be discriminatory or hurtful. Before you show concern about someone's health, which is in and of itself a personal subject, ask yourself what is at the root of your concern. Is it because you have noticed changes or problems with the way this person is acting? It's one thing to show concern for a friend who has suddenly become pale or just had a coughing fit. And it's another thing entirely to ask about a friend's health because he or she is skinnier or fatter than you consider normal.

Similarly, comments about what you should or should not eat can be a code or shorthand for what you are expected to look like. If someone offers you a slice of cake at a birthday party, you might say something such as, "Oh, no thanks. I shouldn't." In most instances, the "shouldn't" isn't because of a health condition like diabetes. It's because you are trying to maintain a certain weight or even lose a little. The phrase "I'm watching what I eat," is code for "watching my weight." People of size get surprising comments and judgments from others based on what they eat. That's easy to avoid doing. But make an effort not to say those things about yourself either. The people around you will take your words as cues that apply to them as well.

A bit of body shaming lurks underneath a compliment or congratulations for someone who has lost weight as well. Though it may seem like a positive thing to tell people that you're impressed or that they look great now that they have lost those fifteen pounds, what that statement reinforces is something negative. Again and again our society rewards those who fit into a narrow definition of

WEIGHT BIAS IN MEDICINE

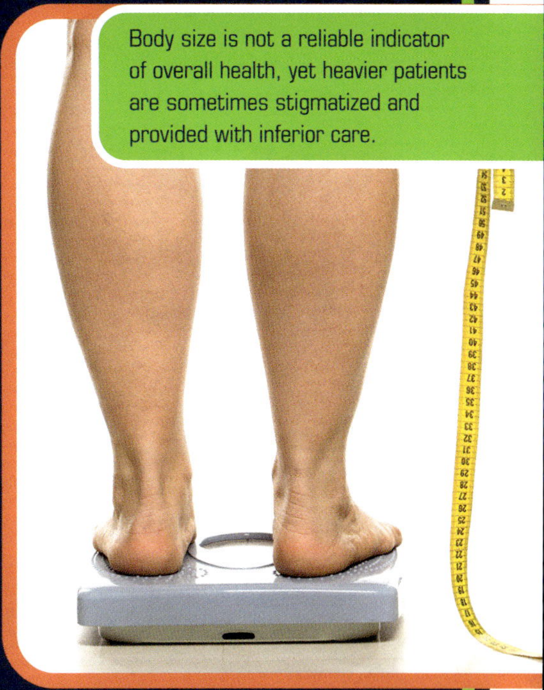

Body size is not a reliable indicator of overall health, yet heavier patients are sometimes stigmatized and provided with inferior care.

Research has shown that doctors and other medical providers are subject to bias against patients they view as overweight or obese. They may assume that heavier patients are generally less healthy. They sometimes view obesity as a failure of willpower and urge patients to lose weight through diet and exercise instead of focusing on their medical concerns. As a result, patients can feel like they're being judged rather than medically evaluated. Weight bias by medical professionals can lead to patients receiving inferior care. Doctors may quickly blame a patient's symptoms on their weight rather than considering other conditions. They may perform more cursory examinations and be less likely to refer them for diagnostic testing. As a result, heavier patients are likelier to suffer from undiagnosed conditions—sometimes even serious conditions such as cancer, thyroid disorders, or heart failure.

Weight bias can harm patients in other ways. Heavier patients are less likely to seek medical care if they believe they will be shamed for their weight. This can lead to patients skipping preventative care screenings that can help ensure lifelong health.

what attractive is. To praise people who previously fell outside of that definition and now have conformed is to reinforce the idea that this is the only way to be attractive.

It feels good to get compliments on your appearance, especially if you have worked hard to diet and exercise to achieve a certain goal. The goal need not be based on your weight, though, but on your mental and physical health and well-being. Getting compliments on your appearance after a recent weight loss sends the message that your "before" body wasn't good enough.

Another reason to avoid praising someone based on a change in weight is that it could have been caused by something other than diet and exercise. There's always a chance that a weight change could be the result of a medical condition or recent illness. This just reinforces the notion that you aren't able to divine someone's health based on appearance.

SHUTTING DOWN SHAMING

There may not be a way to completely prevent all negative conversations around our appearances. We know they come up, so the only way to stop the cycle of body negativity is to learn ways to end or change the conversation. Start

If a friend body shames himself, shift the focus away from his insecurities to something positive about his appearance or abilities.

with yourself: try to stop making negative comments about your own body, even in a joking way. If you compliment someone, don't denigrate yourself in the process. You can tell someone that he or she looks good and leave it at that. Putting yourself down doesn't make the compliment mean more. So, there's no need to compare or measure the appearances of others with yourself.

If someone gives you a backhanded compliment that it looks like you've lost weight or makes a playful remark about the second cookie you ate after dinner, you don't have to respond at all. You can look at the person, acknowledging that you heard what was said, and not say anything back to show that you don't appreciate it. Or, you can ask a simple question to reflect it back to him or her: "Why do you ask?"

If people around you body shame themselves, try to step away from their self-criticism. Don't body shame yourself to try to make someone else feel better. Instead of simply disagreeing, counter with a compliment. Try to refrain from making assumptions about people based on physical characteristics. Body acceptance can help you find qualities to admire in others unrelated to their appearance. You'll feel better about yourself and form stronger connections to the people around you if you reject body shaming.

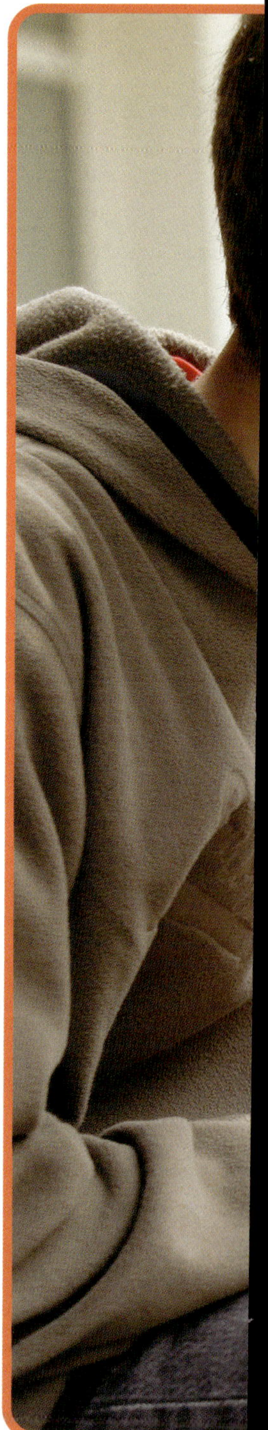

If you want to show your support for a friend, offer a sincere compliment that's not fixated on physical appearance.

CHAPTER 5

LOOKING OUT FOR YOURSELF

Practicing good self-care can help you maintain a positive body image. Self-care goes beyond your body's basic needs, such as nutrition, exercise, and medical care. In addition to your physical well-being, self-care also involves your mental and emotional health. Good self-care habits can help you manage stress, improve your energy level, and boost your self-esteem. It's important that you schedule in time for activities that make you feel good. Practicing gratitude and focusing on positive aspects of your life can also help maintain your mental and emotional well-being. There's a social aspect to self-care too—make sure that you spend time with supportive friends who make you feel good about yourself. If you're in a good place physically, mentally, and emotionally, you'll be better prepared to deal with sources of stress such as body shaming.

SEEKING OUT POSITIVITY

We get messages from many different directions every day telling us what defines an attractive, acceptable, or normal body. The messages come from all sides:

magazines, ads, images on our social media feeds, and the list goes on. Though you can't eliminate all the negative input, you can make conscious decisions to limit some of the influences that you notice having a detrimental effect on your own body image. In order to do that, check in with yourself. If that fitness magazine you subscribe to makes you

Singer-songwriter Taylor Swift poses at a music awards event. Many glamour shots like this one fill the pages of magazines and can perpetuate unrealistic beauty standards.

feel more guilty than inspired, cancel your subscription. If you find yourself comparing your thighs to Taylor Swift's instead of enjoying the celebrity gossip, put down that issue of *People*. You may notice that your friends pick apart the appearances, eating habits, or fitness routines of those around them. Question whether those people care about you as a whole person or if the surface is what they're more interested in.

When you're on social media, what does your feed look like? If it's a sea of diet trends, airbrushed selfies, and fitspiration images, ask yourself if looking at all of that makes you happy. The great thing about any type of social media is that it's personalized. You are the one who chooses which people and organizations to follow. If you come away from perusing your Instagram feed feeling worse about yourself than you did before you checked it, switch it up. Seek out online communities that share your interests, whether it's LGBTQ+ issues or sci-fi fandom. You can make the conscious effort to surround yourself with as many positive messages, influences, and people as you can. Anything (or anyone) that makes you feel your body isn't good enough can be removed with one easy click. Not everything is that simple, so why not make it easy on yourself when you can?

If you're overwhelmed by the negativity of some social media hangouts, try seeking out sites that make you smile and making connections with positive communities.

THE DECEPTIVE SELFIE NOSE

Did you know that your nose typically looks about 6 percent larger in a selfie image? Many people don't realize that a phone camera distorts facial features. In fact, plastic surgeons report receiving more requests for cosmetic surgery due to people wanting to look perfect in the selfies they post on social media. Clients often bring in selfies that have been digitally altered with filters to demonstrate what they want the procedure to achieve. Certain social media trends, such as plastic surgery before and after images, also increase pressure to conform to narrow beauty standards.

If a selfie makes you feel ashamed, remind yourself that digital images don't always reflect reality. Focus on body positivity instead of obsessing over unrealistic ideals.

PROMOTING ACCEPTANCE

Whether you're in a dining hall, locker room, or fitting room, it's hard not to fall into the habit of using negative or judgmental language, especially when you're surrounded by it. But staying body positive will not only keep you feeling good about yourself, it will also help stop the cycle of body shaming among others around you. There are a few key ways you can do this, but at the root of them all is awareness. If you make a conscious effort to recognize body shaming when it occurs around you or on social media and even those negative thoughts you have yourself, you can take steps to make sure you don't perpetuate it.

Gossiping is a fact of our culture and our social lives, but that doesn't mean it's acceptable to make comments about other people's bodies, in front of them or behind their back. If your friends start engaging in this kind of talk, you don't have to participate. Rather, you can say something nice about whomever they are discussing. You can even choose to be direct about the fact that you don't enjoy criticizing people because of their bodies. If you aren't comfortable with either of these options, you

You can create your own social circle of body-positive people, and it will become that much easier to feel comfortable and confident in your own skin.

can stay quiet and just opt out of the conversation entirely. If this type of talk comes up often, these friends may not be the positive influences you want in your inner circle.

Seek out the people who are there for you, who make you feel good about yourself. Those are the friends you want to keep around. Take note of toxic people and influences and see if you can remove them from your life. If it makes you feel bad about your body, you don't need it in your life.

KNOW THEIR PRONOUNS

Most transgender people use pronouns other than the ones they were assigned at birth. Examples of pronoun combinations include he/him, she/her, they/their, he/they, and she/they. For many trans people, their choice of pronouns is an important element of their gender identity, which doesn't always correspond with their gender expression (outward appearance). Using their chosen pronouns indicates acceptance, respect, and affirmation. Using the wrong pronoun—misgendering them—can be hurtful and even offensive. If you inadvertently misgender a person during a conversation, apologize and make an effort to remember their pronouns in the future. If you're not sure of the correct pronouns, ask them. A tactful approach is to introduce yourself by including your own pronouns and then asking which pronouns they prefer. These affirmations can help trans people maintain a positive body image and good mental health.

RESPECTING YOUR BODY

No body is perfect, but rather than focus on imperfections and flaws, concentrate on the things that make you unique and all the great things that your body can do. Everyone has something about their body that they don't like or that they feel particularly insecure about, but it doesn't have to be the main thing you zoom in on every time you look in the mirror. Instead, come up with positive things about your body and focus on those. There will always be things and people in your environment that send negative messages about body image; however, what you tell yourself about your own body is something you can work to improve. Remind yourself that looks aren't everything. Though it's a clichéd phrase, there is also truth to it. There are so many things your body can do and has done. Rather than looking at scars as blemishes, see them as evidence of a challenge you have overcome, testimony of your body's ability to heal itself. Whenever possible, try to take something that you see as a flaw and reframe it into something positive.

Also take note of all the things beyond how your body looks that make you proud to be yourself. Maybe you're a great dancer or you love playing soccer. Appreciate the ways your body can move, your strength, and the things your body does that you may even be proud of.

You can also reframe your goals to reflect how you want to feel rather than how you want to look. Many exercise and diet regimens are centered around the goal of a number on a scale or tape measure. These aren't the types of goals that foster a positive feeling about your body. Change the way you set your goals so that you are focusing on your health—both mental and physical.

Participating in a physical activity that you enjoy can reinforce a positive body image by helping you appreciate your body's capabilities. Believe it or not, regular physical activity is linked to mental health benefits such as boosting your mood and reducing feelings of anxiety and depression. Physical activity doesn't have to be strenuous or painful. Try a few different activities to find out what types you find enjoyable and invigorating. Do you enjoy nature? Try taking regular walks or bike rides. Are you motivated by participating in group activities? Consider joining a fitness class such as yoga or Pilates. Do you prefer solo workouts? Check out online videos for a huge range of options. Are you competitive? Perhaps you would enjoy joining a team. You can start out with small goals and build up to a regular routine. Physical activity, combined with other self-care techniques, can help you maintain body positivity and establish good habits that will provide a good foundation for lifelong health and happiness.

Instead of going running to lose weight, start training for a race. You might be better motivated by improving your running time rather than looking at numbers on a scale.

CHAPTER 6

MOVING PAST BODY SHAMING

It may sometimes seem that incidents of body shaming are impossible to avoid or dismiss. Even the most confident, successful people can be hurt by an unexpected cruel remark about their body. As you have seen, you can take action to improve your body image and strengthen your resilience against body shaming. But the onslaught of shaming from social media and peers can sometimes feel overwhelming, and a negative body image can affect your mental health and behavior.

Body image issues can sap your confidence and affect your everyday activities and your relationships with friends and family. A negative body image can contribute to conditions such as anxiety and depression. Body image issues have also been linked to eating disorders and self-harm. Some people continue struggling with their body image into adulthood. It's important to know when the issue is too serious to deal with on your own and seek help.

EXAMINING YOUR FEELINGS

When you notice instances of body shaming—whether it happens to someone in your social group, on social media, or to you—it is important to be honest about what is happening. If you feel comfortable doing so, confront the person who has done the body shaming. You don't have to be

Body shaming from peers can hurt, but a supportive friend can help keep you grounded about where your priorities really lie.

combative to make it clear what he or she said is not OK. Whether the body shaming is happening to you or someone else, you can say that those words have made you uncomfortable. It doesn't matter who the shamer is talking about because whether the person criticized your looks or someone else's, it's still inappropriate to make those comments. There's a strong chance those comments have made more people uncomfortable than just the person being shamed.

Whether you are able to speak up or not, it is important to examine the effect that body shaming has on you. Even if you don't tell the bully how it made you feel, you still need to acknowledge those feelings for yourself. Has it made you more self-conscious? Has it changed your behavior at all? Think about the way you interact with people and the activities you do. Has anything shifted in the aftermath of body shaming, even if you were just a witness?

Just as your behavior may start to shift in the wake of body shaming, it could happen to a friend or family member just as easily. Just as you can become more observant about when and how body shaming happens, you can also begin recognizing signs when someone in your life is suffering from body shaming's hurtful effects.

TURNING TO FRIENDS

Body shaming should not be dealt with alone. You shouldn't ever feel like you have to keep your feelings to yourself and get past them on your own. Go to someone you trust and can confide in. It is

Try confiding in a friend about your difficulties with body shaming. They may be able to help you view your situation from a different perspective.

likely that this person will do more than just sympathize. He or she likely has a similar experience to share. It will make you feel better to know you are not alone and that you're appreciated.

The person you turn to when you are dealing with body shaming will be someone close to you whom you trust and who will appreciate things about you that you either did not notice or took for granted. They may be about your appearance, like how much this person loves your smile or dimples. But your trusted confidant will probably have reasons deeper than that for why you should feel good about yourself. Maybe you're loyal, good at making people laugh when they've had a bad day, or always able to find the perfect gift. It will be helpful to be reminded of those things. How can you assure yourself of them if you don't even notice them? That's why it's so important to have someone you can turn to.

A friend or family member can stand up for you, comfort you if you're upset, and come up with suggestions and strategies to make you feel better. It is always better to deal with a problem with help. Someone who cares about you will make you feel valued and might take some of the weight and importance away from negative things others may have said about your body.

Therapy can provide an opportunity to work through difficult situations and sort out complicated feelings—including reactions to body shaming.

SEEKING PROFESSIONAL HELP

You may have a good idea of what body shaming is and the many forms it can take, but it can still be hard to tell when you can handle the situation and when it is serious enough that you won't be able to deal with the effects alone. Body shame is very personal, and it may feel embarrassing or even humiliating to go to an adult you may not know very well for help—even with the knowledge that the adult is a trained professional such as a therapist or guidance counselor. You may not know whom to ask in order to find a professional who can help.

If your concern is over a friend, you may be afraid that involving someone else would violate his or her privacy. What if your friend gets mad at you for telling someone else the thoughts and feelings he or she shared with you in confidence? In situations like this, ask yourself a few questions to help assess the severity of the situation.

- Has someone been body shaming your friend on a regular basis?
- Have you noticed changes in your friend's behavior, such as becoming

An obsession with dieting and exercise could indicate an eating disorder. Get help if you think you might have a problem—habits formed in adolescence can be hard to break.

less social, more easily embarrassed, or nervous?
- Have you noticed any changes in his or her eating or exercise habits?

These are merely general questions to help you notice if body shaming has either gotten out of control or had a serious effect on someone you care about.

Though it is a hard choice, it may be more important that this person get the help needed, even if it means he or she gets upset with you for telling someone. Later on, when she or he has more perspective or gets over the initial embarrassment, he or she will hopefully come to understand that you were acting out of concern and care for him or her. If you believe that body shame is changing the way your friend lives his or her life, it is time to get someone involved who is better equipped to handle the problem.

If you are the one being body shamed, and you don't know how to make it stop, it may be time for you to seek outside help for your own well-being. Ask yourself similar questions to the ones you would ask if it were happening to a friend: Have you internalized criticisms of your body and started to think negative thoughts about your body as a result? Have you changed any of your behavior because of body shame? This could be anything from eating habits, to the way you dress, to what activities you feel comfortable participating in. Do you feel more anxious or depressed?

If negative body image interferes with your daily life, contributes to anxiety or depression, or develops into behavior associated with eating disorders, it is time to seek professional help.

Body shame is not something anyone should deal with on their own. Tell a trusted adult, such as a family member, teacher, or guidance counselor, how you have been feeling. This person will either be able to help you or guide you to a trained professional such as a therapist who can work through it with you.

As a teenager, you're subjected to many conflicting pressures as you grow up and establish your unique identity. Body shaming is nothing new for adolescents, but it's harder to ignore for young people today due to the prevalence of social media. As you've seen, there are strategies and resources that can help you cope with the experience of body shaming. If you're comfortable in your own skin, you'll be well prepared to form healthy friendships, approach the world with a confident attitude, and maintain good physical and mental health. You can move past body shaming and thrive with a positive view of your own body.

10 GREAT QUESTIONS TO ASK A COUNSELOR

1. How do I deal with the feelings I have from being body shamed?

2. I think someone may have body shamed me, but I'm not sure. How can I tell if I have been body shamed?

3. My friends or family members tend to make comments on my body that make me feel like it isn't good enough the way it is. What should I do?

4. I have been having negative thoughts about my body or have found myself comparing it with the bodies of other people. How can I control or prevent these thoughts?

5. Someone I know has been body shamed. How can I help him or her?

6. How can I exercise so that it will be enjoyable instead of focusing on changing how I look?

7. How can I work on accepting my body for the way it is today?

8. What can I do to improve my feelings of self-worth and value other aspects about myself besides my appearance?

9. How can I learn to change the conversation with my friends so that it isn't focused on body flaws or exercise and food guilt?

10. Where can I go for help if I'm experiencing an eating disorder or thoughts of self-harm?

In choosing a counselor, look for someone who has experience working with teens regarding relevant issues such as self-esteem or eating disorders.

GLOSSARY

affirmation A statement supporting something known to be true.

amplify To make louder or increase in strength.

androgynous Of unknown sex.

attribute Quality or trait.

capability The power to do something.

combative Prone to getting into fights.

commentary A description or series of opinions regarding a situation or event.

confidant Someone who can be trusted with secrets or private problems.

denigrate To criticize or put down unfairly.

detrimental Tending to cause harm or damage.

discriminatory Referring to the unfair treatment of a person or group based on prejudice toward that person or group.

eating disorder A behavioral condition marked by problems with eating habits and thoughts associated with food.

implicitly Expressed indirectly.

insecurity Self-doubt or a lack of confidence in oneself.

internalize To absorb an opinion, idea, or belief so that it becomes part of how you see yourself.

resilience The ability to recover psychologically after experiencing hardships, trauma, stressful events, or failure.

superficial Shallow or concerned only with surface appearances.

therapist A professional who treats psychological conditions.

validate To demonstrate or support the truth or value of something—a belief, feeling, statement, and so forth.

volatile Threatening to change unpredictably and quickly, usually in a negative direction.

FOR MORE INFORMATION

ABOUT-FACE

2261 Market Street, Suite 139
San Francisco, CA 94114
(415) 448-6263
Website: www.about-face.org
Facebook: @aboutfacesf
Twitter: @aboutfacesf
Instagram: @aboutfacesf
About-Face works to supply women and girls with the tools to resist limiting messages from the media that discourage them from achieving their full potential.

BODY POSITIVE ALLIANCE

Website: bodypositivealliance.org/
Facebook and Instagram: @bodypositivealliance
Twitter: @BoPoAlliance
Body Positive Alliance is a student led nonprofit organization devoted to promoting body positivity through programming events and local clubs or chapters at schools.

MEDIASMARTS

205 Catherine Street, Suite 100
Ottawa, ON K2P 1C3
Canada
(800) 896-3342
Website: mediasmarts.ca

Facebook: @mediasmarts
Twitter: @mediasmarts
Instagram: @mediasmarts.ca
MediaSmarts promotes digital and media literacy among Canadian youth. A discussion of body image can be found at mediasmarts.ca/digital-media-literacy/media-issues/body-image.

MORE THAN A BODY

4140 S 1400 E
Salt Lake City, UT 84124
Website: www.morethanabody.org
Facebook: @beautyredefined
Twitter: @takebackbeauty
Instagram: @beauty_redefined
More Than a Body offers information about body image to help individuals recognize and reject the harmful effects of objectification. The organization provides materials on body resilience through blog posts and social media pages.

NATIONAL EATING DISORDER INFORMATION CENTRE (NEDIC)

ES 7-421, 200 Elizabeth Street
Toronto, ON M5G 2C4
Canada
(866) 633-4220

Website: nedic.ca
Facebook: @thenedic
Twitter: @thenedic
Instagram: @the_nedic
The National Eating Disorder Information Centre (NEDIC) provides Canadians affected by eating disorders with information, resources, referrals, and support.

NATIONAL EATING DISORDERS ASSOCIATION (NEDA)

3308 Preston Road, Suite 350-111
Plano, TX 75093
(800) 931-2237
Website: nationaleatingdisorders.org
Facebook: @NationalEatingDisordersAssociation
Twitter: @NEDAstaff
Instagram: @NEDA
The National Eating Disorders Association (NEDA) supports individuals and families affected by eating disorders through tools such as online screening, resources on treatment options, and a hotline.

NATIONAL WOMEN'S LAW CENTER

11 Dupont Circle NW, Suite 800
Washington, DC 20036
(202) 588-5180
Website: nwlc.org
Facebook: @NWLC

Twitter: @NWLC
Instagram: @nationalwomenslawcenter
The National Women's Law Center advocates for the rights of girls and women in public policy, the courts, and society. Their 2018 publication, "Dress Coded: Black girls, bodies, and bias in D.C. schools" examined harmful preconceptions about bodies and clothing.

PSYCHOLOGY TODAY

115 East 23rd Street, 9th Floor
New York, NY 10010
Website: www.psychologytoday.com/
Facebook: @psychologytoday
Instagram: @psych_today
Twitter: @psychtoday
Psychology Today is a magazine and online site fousing on psychology and mental health. It provides resources on issues such as body shaming, as well as listings for mental health professionals.

FOR FURTHER READING

Dick, Emily Lauren. *Body Positive: A Guide to Loving Your Body*. Sanger, CA: Familius, 2020.

Fairchild, Melody. *Girls Running: All You Need to Strive, Thrive, and Run Your Best*. Boulder, CO: VeloPress, 2020.

Green, Meghan. *Body Image and Body Shaming*. New York, NY: Lucent Press, 2017.

Hugstad, Kristi. *Be You, Only Better: Real-Life Self-Care for Young Adults (and Everyone Else)*. Novato, CA: New World Library, 2021.

Markey, Charlotte N. *Being You: The Body Image Book for Boys*. Cambridge, UK: Cambridge University Press, 2022.

Markey, Charlotte N. *The Body Image Book for Girls: Love Yourself and Grow Up Fearless*. Cambridge, UK: Cambridge University Press, 2021.

Orr, Tamra B. *Combatting Body Shaming*. New York, NY: Rosen Publishing Group, 2017.

Skeen, Michelle. *Just as You Are: A Teen's Guide to Self-Acceptance and Lasting Self-Esteem*. Oakland, CA: New Harbinger Publications, Inc., 2018.

Stanley, Jessamyn. *Every Body Yoga: Let Go of Fear, Get on the Mat, Love Your Body*. New York, NY: Workman Publishing, 2017.

Thomas, Bonnie. *Creative Coping Skills for Teens and Tweens: Activities for Self Care and Emotional Support Through Art, Yoga and Mindfulness*. Philadelphia, PA: Jessica Kingsley Publishers, 2019.

INDEX

J

K

M

N

P

R

ABOUT THE AUTHOR

ROSE MCCARTHY

Rose McCarthy is an author who has written numerous books for children and young adults. Several have addressed social and legal issues faced by teens. She lives in New York.

PHOTO CREDITS

Photo credits: cover Eviart/Shutterstock.com; cover, pp. 1–80 STUDIO DREAM/Shutterstock.com; cover, p. 1 HIGOOD/Shutterstock.com; p. 6 Shift Drive/Shutterstock.com; p. 7 Diablo Gato/Shutterstock.com; p. 9 Tinseltown/Shutterstock.com; p. 11 LightField Studios/Shutterstock.com; p. 13 https://commons.wikimedia.org/wiki/File:Marilyn_Monroe_at_Ciro%27s.jpg; p. 15 Dejan Dundjerski/Shutterstock.com; pp. 17, 24 Prostock-studio/Shutterstock.com; p. 19 Samuel Borges Photography/Shutterstock.com; p. 21 Christian Bertrand/Shutterstock.com; p. 23 wavebreakmedia/Shutterstock.com; p. 26 javiii23/Shutterstock.com; p. 29 PR Image Factory/Shutterstock.com; p. 31 LADO/Shutterstock.com; p. 32 Kathy Hutchins/Shutterstock.com; pp. 35, 51 Rawpixel.com/Shutterstock.com; p. 37 Artem Varnitsin/Shutterstock.com; pp. 39, 59 BearFotos/Shutterstock.com; p. 41 Vladimir Gjorgiev/Shutterstock.com; p. 43 Leszek Glasner/Shutterstock.com; p. 45 Phovoir/Shutterstock.com; p. 47 DFree/Shutterstock.com; p. 49 wong yu liang/Shutterstock.com; p. 55 New Africa/Shutterstock.com; p. 57 Lopolo/Shutterstock.com; p. 61 BAZA Production/Shutterstock.com; p. 62 Surasak_Photo/Shutterstock.com; p. 64 VGstockstudio/Shutterstock.com; p. 67 spb2015/Shutterstock.com.